# Stamping
*made easy*

# Stamping
## made easy

### Series Editors: Susan & Martin Penny

David & Charles

A DAVID & CHARLES BOOK

VP VRW

First published in the UK in 1998

A catalogue record for this book is available from the British Library.

ISBN 0 7153 0565 4

Series Editors: Susan & Martin Penny
Designed by Penny & Penny
Illustrations: Fred Fieber at Red Crayola
Photography: Ashton James; Jon Stone
Stylist: Susan Penny

Printed in France by Imprimerie Pollina S. A.
for David & Charles
Brunel House  Newton Abbot  Devon

# Contents

# Introduction to Stamping

*Stamping Made Easy* is a complete guide to the craft of stamping; very little specialist equipment is needed when stamping, and most of the stamps used in this book are made from everyday items: kitchen scourers, clothes pegs, cork tiles, leaves and fruit, making stamping one of the cheapest and easiest craft techniques

## Essential Equipment

Here is a list of the equipment needed when stamping:

- **Paper** – use copier paper to make a tracing of the design.
- **Cutting mat** – a mat that self heals when cut and will protect your work surface.
- **Cutting knife** – slim craft knife, sharp enough to carve sponge or foam and to cut rubber erasers, cork and polystyrene tiles.
- **Artist's paintbrush** – used to coat the surface of a stamp with paint.
- **Decorator's paintbrush** – used to apply a wash, base coat or varnish to wood.
- **Foam roller** – used for rolling paint on to the surface of a stamp.
- **Paint dish** – flat plastic microwave dish or fresh food tray.
- **Kitchen paper** – useful for mopping up spills and cleaning stamps.
- **Cotton buds** – used to clean stamps.
- **Cotton wool** – used to clean stamps.
- **Cocktail stick** – used for mixing paint.
- **Fine sandpaper** – use for rubbing down wooden surfaces before stamping.
- **Toaster** – for melting embossing powder when applied to paper.
- **Masking tape** – use strips as a guide for stamping.
- **Corrugated card** – a base for mounting cork, polystyrene, string and leaves.
- **Wooden blocks** – a base for mounting foam sheet, or string.

## Tips for stamping on paper

- ✔ Do not overload the paper with paint
- ✔ Leave the stamped paper to dry flat
- ✔ Use acrylic and emulsion paint on paper
- ✔ Add detail to a stamped image with a thick nibbed felt-tipped pen
- ✔ Stamp lining paper to make inexpensive gift wrap
- ✔ Use embossing ink and powder to add an extra dimension to paper

## Tips for stamping on fabric

- ✔ Wash to remove 'finishing' and shrinkage
- ✔ Test the paint on the fabric, for bleeding
- ✔ Fix fabric paint with an iron after stamping
- ✔ Cover fabric that you are not working on with paper, to keep it clean

- ✔ Stick masking tape strips, or lengths of lining paper to the fabric, and use as guides
- ✔ Some fabric paint will be too thin for stamping: add stencil paint to thicken

## Making Stamps

Below is a list of items from which you can make stamps:

- **Cork floor tiles** – thin floor tile made from closely packed cork.
- **Washing-up sponge** – use a firm sponge or kitchen scourer.
- **Packing foam** – a sheet of white foam.
- **Potato** – half a large baking potato.
- **Rubber eraser** – pre-shaped rubbers or stamps cut from rubber erasers.
- **Wooden clothes peg** – remove the metal spring from a clothes peg, then use the flat wooden end as a stamp.

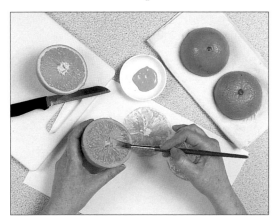

- **Fruit** – any firm skinned fruit or vegetable with an interesting internal structure.
- **Leaves** – fresh, green leaves with pronounced veins.
- **Plastic cotton reels** – use the spokes at the end of a cotton reel to stamp wheels on vehicles.
- **String** – stick coiled string to cardboard.
- **Corks** – use wine bottle corks.
- **Hands** – dip your hands in paint, then walk them across the project surface.
- **Foam rubber block** – carve stamps from tightly packed high-density foam.
- **Polystyrene tile** – cut shapes from ceiling tiles then stick to mount board.

## Choosing the right paint

Choosing the right paint for the right surface can be difficult: listed below are some of the plus and minus points to help you make that choice.

- **Acrylic** – Water-based
  - The right consistency for stamping
  - Colours can be mixed
  - Large range of colours available
  - Will give good results on most surfaces
  - Brushes can be washed in water
  - Dries fast
  - Use water-based varnish to seal
- **Emulsion** – Water-based
  - Sold in small tester pots
  - Mostly pale colours, but can be mixed
  - Use as a base coat for stamping on to
- **Ceramic** – Water-based
  - Use on china, ceramics and tiles
  - Will air-dry in 72 hours
  - High gloss finish
  - Can be used on bathroom tiles
  - Most are dishwasher safe on china
- **Fabric paint** – Water-based
  - Some makes too thin for stamping
  - Colours can be mixed
  - Test for 'bleeding'
  - Brushes can be washed in water
  - Iron fix before laundering
- **Matt acrylic varnish** – Water-based
  - Brush and spray-on
  - Wash brushes in water
  - No smell and dries very quickly
- **Polyurethane varnish** – Oil-based
  - Brush-on, very slow to dry
  - Wash brushes in white spirit
  - Work in a well ventilated room
  - Very tough finish
- **Stamping ink**
  - Use an ink pad to load the stamp
  - Used mainly with ready-made stamps
  - Difficult to clean up spills
- **Embossing ink**
  - Use an ink pad to load the stamp
  - Glue – not paint or ink
  - Used only under embossing powder
  - Holds powder to project until melted

# Making Stamps

Almost any object with one flat surface can be used to make a stamp. It must have an interesting shape, surface or internal structure, and be able to transfer paint to the project surface. Stamps need not be expensive: organic material like fruit and leaves can make some very interesting stamped shapes

## Using corks & clothes pegs

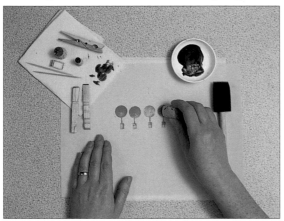

Almost any object, as long as it has a flat side, can be used to stamp. The end of a wooden clothes peg will make a rectangular shape, whereas a cork makes a mottled circle.

## Using rubber erasers

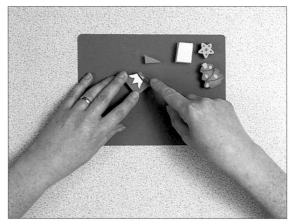

Stamp with pre-shaped rubbers or cut your own design from a rubber eraser: attach a paper pattern to the rubber, then cut around the edge using a sharp craft knife.

## Using string

Draw spirals and coils on to corrugated card. Glue along the drawn lines, then lay string over the glue. Cut off the excess string. Trim the card just larger than the string shape.

## Using foam rubber block

High-density foam rubber block makes a good stamp. Make a tracing of the design, then pin to the foam. Cut away the excess foam, leaving the design as a raised block.

## Using leaves

Place a leaf on to mount board or card. Using a ball-point pen, trace around the leaf. Cut out the shape inside the drawn lines, so that the card is very slightly smaller than the leaf. Glue the top side of the leaf to the card shape. Glue a small piece of mount board to the card to act as a handle.

## Using your hands

Place the paint next to the fabric, and have kitchen paper handy so that you can wipe your hands easily. Place your hand in the paint, making sure every part is well covered: use a brush to add more paint if needed. Press your hand firmly on the fabric, then remove carefully.

## Using potatoes

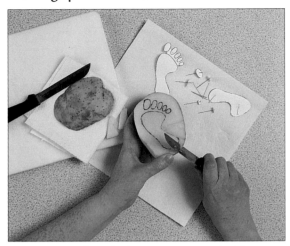

Cut a large firm baking potato in half lengthways. Dry the cut surface, then place on kitchen paper to soak up any excess fluid. Pin a design tracing to the surface of the potato, then draw around it with felt-tipped pen. Cut away the potato outside the drawn lines, to a depth of 1cm (³⁄₈in).

## Using sponge

Make a paper template of the design, then pin the template to the top of a washing-up sponge. Using sharp scissors carefully cut the sponge to the same size as the template. The sponge will soak up the paint making it difficult to clean, so make a stamp for each paint colour used.

## Using a cotton reel

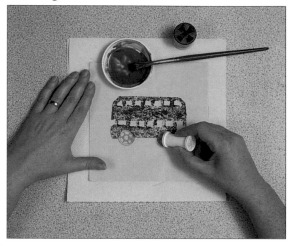

To make wheels on a stamped vehicle, use the end of a cotton reel: remove the paper circle from the end of a plastic cotton reel to reveal the 'spokes'. Apply paint to the spokes, using a paintbrush. Gently press the cotton reel on to the stamped vehicle. Re-apply the paint before stamping again.

## Using fruit

Using a sharp knife and working on a clean chopping board, cut a piece of fruit in half then lay cut side down on kitchen paper to absorb the juice. Use a paint brush or roller to coat the fruit with paint. Firm skinned fruits or vegetables, with an interesting internal structure, make the best stamps.

## Using cork tiles

Make a paper template of your design, then lay the template on to a cork tile. Draw around the shape with a ball-point pen, then cut using a sharp craft knife or scissors. Cut a piece of stiff cardboard slightly larger than the cork shape. Using PVA glue, stick the cork shape to its cardboard backing.

## Using foam sheet

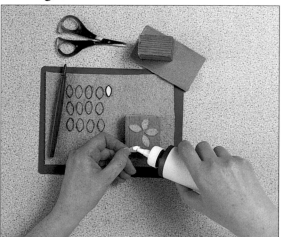

Lay petal-shaped paper templates on to a sheet of packing foam, draw around the shapes with a felt-tipped pen. Using craft scissors cut out the foam petals. Sand down the surface of a block of wood, then using craft glue stick six or eight petals firmly on to the top of the block, forming a circle.

# Stamping Techniques

Stamping is just a matter of transferring paint or ink to the project surface; but how you load the paint and how much you use will change the look of the stamped image. Too much paint and the image will fill in; too little and it will be broken. Here we help you find the right method

## *Loading the stamp pad*

Stamping or embossing ink should be applied to a stamp from a pad. Spread the ink over the pad using a sponge brush: allow the ink to soak into the pad before using.

## *Loading the stamp*

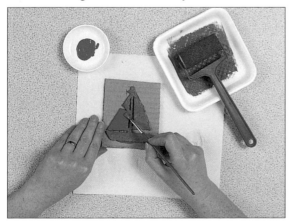

Use a brush to apply paint to the surface of a stamp; if you are using the stamp repeatedly, a roller will be quicker to use and gives a very even paint application.

## *Embossing*

Load an ink pad with embossing ink, press the stamp on to the ink then stamp firmly on to paper. Before the ink dries, sprinkle embossing powder liberally on the ink. Leave for a few seconds then carefully shake off the excess powder.

Hold the stamped paper over the top of a heated toaster for a few seconds to melt the embossing powder. Do not overheat the powder, or it will lose its shine.

# Hints and Tips

Good preparation is important when stamping, if you want a professional finish. Keeping your equipment and stamps clean will ensure that paint only goes where it's intended; and if a spill does occur, then kitchen roll is invaluable for clearing it up

### Preparing your work surface

Before you begin stamping, cover your work surface with clean lining paper. Keep all your equipment close at hand, and clean water and kitchen paper to mop up any stray paint.

### Working on wood

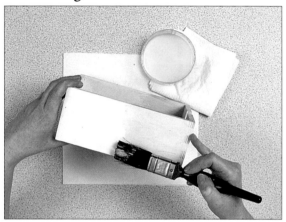

To colour bare wood before stamping: sand the surface of the wood, then wipe with a damp cloth. When dry, paint with several coats of acrylic paint thinned with water.

### Preparing for painting

Always prepare surfaces before stamping: use fine sand paper on wood; scrub terracotta flower pots in warm soapy water; and launder fabric to remove any 'finishing'.

### Applying varnish to wood

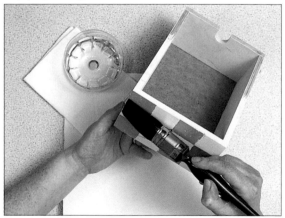

Seal the surface of stamped wood with two coats of matt or satin varnish to protect it from dirty marks. Use acrylic varnish on water-based paint and polyurethane on oil.

## Working on fabric

Always test the paint on the fabric before you begin stamping: some paint will soak into the fabric rapidly; others will let the paint 'bleed' into the weave. Depending on your test, you may need to thin down the paint with a little water; or thicken it with fabric or stencil paint of a similar colour.

## Fixing fabric paint

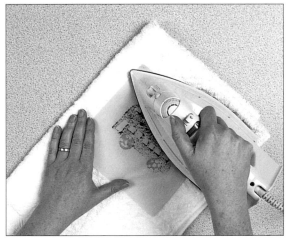

Leave fabric paint to dry, then heat to fix the paint. Cover the fabric with a cotton cloth; or place it face down on a fluffy towel. Iron for 1-2 minutes on the hottest setting suitable for the fabric. Although most fabric paint is heat-fixed, read the manufacturer's instructions before proceeding.

## Working on tiles

Almost any paint can be used on untreated terracotta floor tiles, as long as they are sealed first with emulsion paint; on shiny glazed tiles, use a water-based cold-set ceramic paint. This will air-dry in about 72 hours, and its high gloss finish is waterproof enough to use in the bathroom.

## Cleaning your stamps

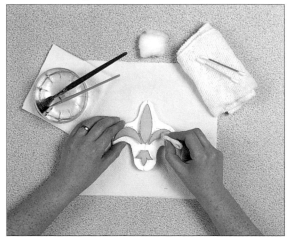

It is important to keep all your equipment clean when stamping. Wipe the stamp between each colour change and at regular intervals when in use. On water-based paints, use cotton wool or a cotton bud dipped in water; on oil paints use white spirit. Dry the stamp thoroughly before re-using.

# Fruit Printed Bags and Paper

There's no need to make a special stamp for this project, as the
shapes used on these bags are all stamped with real fruit. These
hand-made bags are quick and easy to stamp and can be made
from lining paper, costing you next to nothing to make

## You will need

- Sheets of white or cream paper, lining paper
- Fruit – orange, lemon, lime, star fruit
- Acrylic or poster paint – green, yellow, orange
- Cord – for the handles
- Raffia, wool or string – for the tassel
- Card – small piece to make the tassel
- Book – to use as a pattern for the gift bag
- Double-sided tape
- Hole punch
- Chopping board, sharp knife
- Paint brush or foam roller
- Flat dish for paint
- Container of clean water
- Kitchen paper
- Scrap paper
- Scissors

## Preparing the fruit

1 Almost any citrus fruit can be used as a
stamp: the fruit should have a firm skin and
an interesting internal structure. Vegetables
can also be used as stamps: try using peppers,
tomatoes or aubergines printed in hot spicy
colours.

2 Using a sharp knife and working on a
chopping board, cut the fruit in half and
lay the pieces cut side down on kitchen paper
to absorb the juice.

## Stamping with fruit

1 Pour a small quantity of paint into a dish.
Load the roller with paint then coat the cut
surface of a piece of fruit, making sure the
paint is not too thick; or use a paint brush to
coat the surface of the fruit, taking care to
apply the paint evenly.

2 To achieve the best results, practise
stamping on scrap paper before you start the
project. Position the fruit on to the paper and
press down firmly and evenly. Remove carefully
to prevent the paint from smudging
(see Making Stamps, page 8). You may have to
increase or reduce the paint on the stamp
depending on the imprint left on the paper.
The stamp may need to be loaded with paint
between each print; or it may only need loading
after a few applications. This will depend on

the thickness of the paint; the absorbency of the paper and the natural moisture in the fruit.

3 On white paper or lining paper begin stamping: use different combinations of shapes and colours on each sheet of paper. Apply the fruit stamps randomly or in uniform rows to create interesting patterns. Leave to dry.

## Making the gift bag

1 You can make just about any size of gift bag, but you will need a book to use as a pattern, over which to create the bag. Wrap a piece of stamped paper around a book, overlapping the ends, adding approximately 2.5cm (1in) to each edge.

2 Spread the paper flat on the table, fold over one long edge, holding it in place with double-sided tape. This will be the top edge when the bag is assembled.

3 Wrap the paper around the book, with the folded top edge lined up with the top of the book. Secure the overlapped side edge with double-sided tape. Leave the top folded end open.

4 At the bottom end, fold in each corner of the paper, as you would when wrapping a

present. Secure with double sided tape. Crease the paper bag on each of the edges of the book.

5 Slide the book out of the bag. Flatten the bag bringing the side edges together – this will create a 'v' shaped indentation on each side of the bag.

6 Punch holes on the top edge of the bag: two on the front side and two corresponding on the back.

7 For the handles, cut two lengths of cord. Thread the cord through the holes in the bag, knotting the thread ends inside the bag.

## Making the tassels

1 Wind a length of raffia, wool or string around a short piece of card about 4cm (1½in) wide, twenty or thirty times.

2 Slip a length of raffia, wool or string through the loops at one end of the card. Knot the thread to hold the loops tightly together.

3 Holding the thread tightly on the card, cut through the loops at the bottom end of the card. Carefully remove the card, still holding the cut ends together.

4 Tie a length of raffia, wool or string around the cut loops about 1cm (³/₈in) from the top. Trim across the cut ends to neaten.

5 Slip a long length of raffia, wool or string through the top of the tassel and attach it to a parcel or gift bag.

## Stamping the fruit tags

1 Stamp a fruit shape on to paper. Leave to dry. Cut around the outer edge of the fruit.

2 Punch a hole in the top, thread with string or raffia.

3 Alternatively, make a folded tag with the fruit shape stamped on either side. Stamp two fruit shapes close together.

4 When dry, cut around both shapes leaving a small paper bridge between the two. Fold on the paper bridge, bringing the fruit shapes together. Stamp a hole in the top and thread with string or raffia.

5 Fill the present bag with shredded tissue paper, then tie the fruit stamped tag to the top of the bag.

# Trains, Boats and Planes Quilt

This fun quilt cover, made from easy-to-wash cotton, can be quickly pieced together from stamped squares. Use the same stamped fabric to cover a storage box; or use acrylic paint to stamp the tractor, train, bus, plane, boat and car on the wall – a great way to co-ordinate the nursery decor!

## You will need

- Cotton fabric 1.5mx140cm wide (1⅝ydx54in), plus enough to cover the box and lid – yellow; 50x140cm wide (20x54in) – blue
- Hat or storage box
- Ribbon, to fit around the hat box
- Fabric paints – yellow, navy blue, white
- Thin cork tile 30x30cm (12x12in)
- Stiff cardboard to make the stamp mounts
- Plastic cotton reels – large and small
- Cardboard template – 17x17cm (7x7in)
- White paper, ball-point pen, pencil
- Craft knife, cutting mat, craft and fabric scissors
- Matching sewing thread, pins, poppers or ties for the duvet
- PVA glue, masking tape
- Lining paper to cover your work surface
- Flat dishes for mixing paint, container of clean water, small paintbrush, kitchen paper
- Sewing machine
- Iron, fluffy towel

## Making the stamp

1 Trace over the vehicle designs on page 22 and 23 on to white paper with a pencil. Carefully cut around the lines to produce a paper template for each.

2 Lay the templates on to the cork tile, and holding firmly on the surface, draw around each, using a ball-point pen. You can change the direction of the vehicle by reversing the template. You will be able to get quite a few stamps out of one tile, by turning the vehicles around, then fitting them together like a jigsaw puzzle.

3 Using a craft knife and cutting mat or scissors, cut out the cork vehicles. If you cut the cork incorrectly, mend the break with glue.

4 Roughly cut pieces of stiff cardboard slightly larger than each of the stamp shapes. Using PVA glue stick a cork vehicle to its cardboard backing. Leave the glue to dry.

## Preparing the fabric

1 Lay the square cardboard template on to the fabric, draw around the outer edge with a pencil, then cut out the squares: eighteen yellow and seventeen blue.

2 From the yellow fabric, cut a rectangle 77x107cm (31x43in) for the quilt back.

## Applying the stamp

1 Cover your working surface with lining paper to protect it. Mix the navy blue, yellow and white fabric paints in different quantities to produce six shades of blues and greens: always add a small amount of the darker colour to the lighter colour, this will stop you making the shades too dark. To complete the project you will need to mix approximately one dessert spoon of each colour, keeping each colour in a separate dish.

2 Lay a square of the yellow fabric, right side up, on the work surface. Apply the fabric paint to the cork stamp with a small paint brush, using a different colour for each stamp. Do not let the paint accumulate in the cutaway sections, or this will fill in and spoil the definition of the design.

3 Press the stamp firmly on to the fabric and remove gently so as not to smudge the paint, or lift up the fabric. If necessary practise on a scrap of fabric until you feel confident applying the stamp. Keep your hands and brushes clean. Remember to allow for the addition of any wheels when positioning the stamp within the square. Stamp three squares with each of the six designs. Leave to dry flat.

4 To stamp the vehicle wheels: remove the paper circles from the end of the plastic cotton reels to reveal the 'spokes'. Lay the stamped square requiring the wheels, right side up, on folded kitchen paper. Apply paint to the spokes at the end of the reel, then gently press on to the fabric. Use the photograph on page 21 for colouring and positioning the wheels. Repeat for the other vehicles. Leave to dry flat.

5 To fix the fabric paint: place the stamped squares painted side down on a fluffy towel, and iron for 1-2 minutes on a cotton setting.

## Making the duvet

1 Pin, then tack, alternate yellow and blue squares, as shown in the diagram below, taking a 1cm ($^3$/$_8$in) seam allowance. Machine stitch along each seam, then trim and neaten using a zig-zag stitch. It is easier to assemble the patchwork if you join the rows across the duvet, then stitch the strips together.

Use this layout diagram as a guide when assembling your duvet front; or you may prefer to assemble the stamped squares randomly.

2 Lay the pieced front, right sides together, on top of the yellow fabric cut for the duvet back. Stitch up the sides and across the top, taking a seam allowance of 1cm ($^3$/$_8$in). Trim

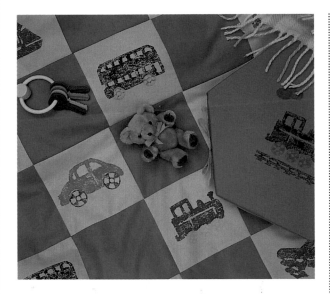

and neaten the seam, inside the bag, with a zig-zag stitch. Turn over the bottom edge of the bag twice, while it is inside out. Pin, tack, then machine stitch around the edge. Turn the bag through to the right side, then press. Attach poppers or ties to the bottom edge of the duvet cover, to hold the duvet in place.

## Making up the box

1 Measure the height and circumference of the box base. Add enough fabric to allow for an overlap, and about 2.5cm (1in) for turning inside and on to the bottom of the box. Cut the fabric and wrap around the box base, then mark the stamping positions on the fabric using pins. Remember to put the lid on the box, to position the stamps low enough, so as not to disappear under the lid.

2 Stamp each vehicle on the cut fabric, in the same way as for the duvet, but with the addition of the detail stamps: sea, grass, rails and road beneath the vehicles; sun and clouds above. Refer to the main photograph for position.

3 Cut a piece of blue fabric, large enough to wrap over the box lid, adding 2.5cm (1in)

for gluing inside the lid. Mark the centre point of the fabric, then stamp your chosen vehicle, and detail on to the fabric. Leave to dry flat.

4 To fix the fabric paint: place the stamped fabric side and top, painted side down on a fluffy towel, and iron for 1-2 minutes on a cotton setting.

5 Spread glue over the box sides, and about 2.5cm (1in) inside the box and about the same amount on to the box bottom. Lay the fabric painted side down on to your work surface. Roll the box on to the fabric, making sure the stamped vehicles are in the correct position. To neaten the fabric join on the box side: turn the overlapping fabric under, so that it just overlaps the other fabric end, which is already stuck to the box. Glue in place.

6 Turn the fabric over at the top of the box on to the glue inside; make small cuts in the fabric to ease it in place. Turn the excess fabric, at the bottom of the box, over on to the glue base; if the fabric will not sit flat on the bottom, make small cuts in the fabric, adding more glue where the fabric overlaps.

7 Repeat for the lid, taking care to position the stamped vehicle in the centre of the lid. Glue ribbon around the edge of the box lid, making a small flat bow to cover the join.

8 Neaten the fabric edge inside the box, with a continuous strip of masking tape stuck carefully over the raw edge. Repeat for the lid. Use smaller strips to cover the raw fabric edge on the base.

Sea

Railway

Grass

Clouds

Use these designs to cut your own vehicle stamps
from a cork tile.

Sun

Road

# Fishy Tiles

These fun fish tiles will bring a touch of the Mediterranean to any bathroom. Stamped using a cold-set ceramic paint, these bright cheerful tiles in orange and yellow, then hand-finished in red and blue, are waterproof enough to be used in most bathroom situations

The fish stamp is cut from a block of high-density foam rubber, which can be purchased from an upholstery supplies shop. This tightly packed foam will give a crisp finish, when the paint is stamped on to the surface of the tiles.

## You will need

- Plain glazed ceramic tiles
- Cold-set ceramic paint, water-based – orange, white, red, yellow, blue
- High-density foam rubber block
- Craft knife, cutting mat, scissors, metal ruler
- White paper, pencil, pins
- Flat dish for mixing paint, container of clean water, fine paintbrush, foam roller, cocktail stick

## Making the stamp

1 Using a craft knife and cutting mat, cut a piece of foam rubber the same size as your tiles.

2 Trace over the fish design on page 27 on to white paper with a pencil. Carefully cut out the fish tracing from the paper.

3 Position the fish tracing on the centre of the foam rubber. Push pins through the paper into the foam, to hold it in place.

4 Place the foam on a cutting mat. Using a craft knife, carefully cut away the foam from around the edge of the fish shape, leaving the fish on a raised block – only cut away about half of the depth of the foam.

5 To make the wavy stamp: cut a rectangular block of foam the width of a tile. Make a tracing of the wavy shape, pin to the foam block, then cut away the excess foam, leaving a raised block as before.

## Applying the stamp

1 The tiles used in the project are very shiny, making it difficult for paint to adhere to and so stay on the surface. Water-based cold-set ceramic paint, which will air-dry in about 72 hours, has a high gloss finish making it waterproof and so usable in most bathroom

situations. Do read the paint manufacturer's instructions carefully, as not all cold-set ceramic paints have these special qualities.

2 Pour a quantity of orange cold-set ceramic paint on to a flat dish. Load a foam roller with paint, then roll the paint evenly on to the fish stamp; or you may prefer to press the stamp directly into the paint. Hold the stamp just above the tile, carefully aligning the edges of the foam block with the tile. Press the stamp very firmly down on to the tile. Remove the stamp, taking care not to move the stamp or tile, or the image will be smudged. When changing paint colours, you will need to wash and dry your equipment thoroughly before moving on to the next colour.

3 Pour a quantity of yellow cold-set ceramic paint on to a flat dish, and load the wavy stamp as before. Align the stamp with the top of the tile, then press it firmly down on to the tile, transferring the wavy shape. Leave the tiles to dry thoroughly, for about 72 hours. If the images are too faint you may want to re-stamp them. This should only be done when the paint is completely dry, and if great care is taken when positioning the stamp; if possible try to get a strong enough image with the first stamp.

## Painting the detail

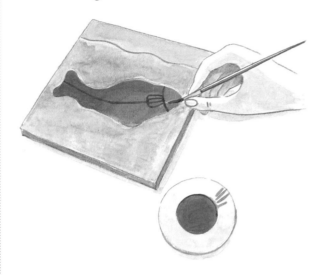

1 Once the main shapes are dry they can be overpainted with the detail. Mix a little orange and red paint together, using a cocktail stick. Paint the fish scales, fins and mouth using a fine paintbrush and the orangey/red paint, following the diagram opposite. Add a white dot for the fish eye.

2 Using the same orangey/red paint and the fine paintbrush, add a row of evenly spaced swirls on the yellow wavy band at the top of the tile.

3 Paint two thin blue waves on the bottom of each tile, using a fine paintbrush. Add a dot of blue to the centre of each fish eye.

4 Leave the tiles to dry. After 72 hours they can be fixed to the wall and grouted. Do read the paint manufacturer's instructions carefully, as some makes of paint can be affected by the grout or the tile adhesive.

**Use this fish and wave design to make your stamps. Paint the detail lines by hand when the stamped image has completely dried.**

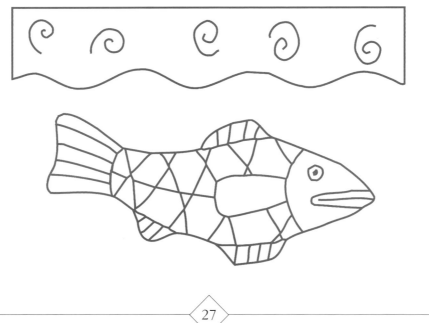

# Harlequin Christmas

This special Harlequin Christmas set will look spectacular on and around your tree. The easy-to-make tree tub cover will hide that old flowerpot, and the chair covered in bright jewel-like colours is a warm invitation for Santa, to rest and enjoy a glass of sherry

## You will need

- Dupion silk for the tub, stocking, bag and chair ties, 1.5mx90cm (1⅝ydx36in) – purple
- Dupion silk for the tub and chair skirt, 2.3mx90cm (2½ydx36in) – red
- Dupion silk for the stocking, chair cover, 1.3mx90cm (1⅜ydx36in) – blue
- Ribbon 2.5cm (1in) wide, tub top – gold
- Ribbon 2.5cm (1in) wide, pouch – red
- Ribbon 6mm (¼in) wide to hang the tree decorations – red and blue
- Felt 1mx90cm (1⅛ydx36in) – white
- Beads 1.2cm (½in) – thirty gold; four red
- Cord 1.80m (2yd) and tassel – gold
- Thin card – white, matt gold, red
- Tissue paper – red, blue
- Cork floor tiles, fine
- Fabric paint – gold; relief paint – red
- Embossing ink – clear
- Embossing powder – gold, blue
- Cabochon jewellery stones
- Craft knife, cutting mat, decorator's paintbrush,
- Matching sewing thread
- All-purpose glue, fabric glue
- Toaster, iron, fluffy towel, paperclips, ball-point pen

## Making the stamp

1 Trace over the curl, small and large holly leaves, small and large crowns, and small and large dove designs on pages 32 to 35 on to white paper with a pencil. Carefully cut around the lines to produce a paper template for each.

2 Lay the templates on the smooth side of the cork tile, and holding firmly on the surface, draw around each using a ball-point pen.

3 Lay the tile on a cutting mat and using a craft knife, cut out the cork shapes.

## Stamping the tree tub cover

1 Cut a strip of thin card just higher than and large enough to fit around your Christmas tree tub, adding a 7.5cm (3in) overlap. Cut a length of purple dupion the same size, adding 2.5cm (1in) on all sides for turnings.

2 Lay the dupion flat on to a clean work surface. Using a paint brush, apply a thin coat of gold fabric paint to the crown stamp and press firmly and at random on to the fabric. Keep 2.5cm (1in) above the lower long edge and 10cm (4in) below the upper.

3 Place the dupion face down on a fluffy towel and iron for 1-2 minutes to fix the fabric paint. Do not have the iron too hot or it will scorch the fabric.

4 Using the tube of red relief paint, apply a dot on the end of each crown point. Leave to dry.

5 Make a paper pattern of the stocking cuff on page 32, repeating the design until it fits across the top of the tree tub. Pin the pattern on to the red dupion and cut two cuffs.

6 Paint the curl stamp with gold paint and press on to each point on one of the red cuffs; refer to the diagram on page 32 for the position. Leave to dry. Fix the paint with an iron as before.

7 With right sides facing and taking a 1cm (³⁄₈in) seam allowance, stitch the red cuffs together along the zig-zag lower edge. Trim the seam allowance at the points and snip to the inner corners. Turn right side out and press, tack the upper raw edges together. Sew a bead on each point.

8 Lay the stamped purple dupion right side up on the card tree tub, matching the upper edges. Glue the fabric to the upper edge of the card. Glue the lower edge and sides of the fabric to the reverse side of the card.

9 Lay the cuff on the covered tree tub, matching the top edges. Glue together along the top edge of the tub, glue gold ribbon along the top to cover the raw edges. Wrap the stamped cover around the tree base, then fix with paper clips.

## Stamping the stocking

1 Make a paper pattern of the stocking on page 34, then cut two stockings from blue dupion.

2 Stamp the small dove using gold paint on to one of the stocking pieces, see page 34 for position. Leave to dry then fix the paint.

3 With the right sides facing and taking a 1cm (³⁄₈in) seam allowance, stitch the stocking pieces together. Snip the curves and turn right side out. To hang the stocking: sew a folded length of red ribbon to the top.

4 Make a paper template using the cuff diagram on page 32, add enough sections to fit around the top of the stocking. Cut two cuffs from purple dupion, then stamp in gold paint with the small holly leaf on to each point of the cuff. Leave to dry, then fix with the iron.

5 With the right sides facing and taking a 1cm (³⁄₈in) seam allowance, stitch the short ends of each cuff together. With the right sides facing, place one cuff inside the other and stitch along the lower zig-zag edge.

6 Trim the points and snip to the inner corners, then turn right side out and press. Tack the upper raw edges together. Slip the cuff inside the stocking matching the right side of the cuff to the wrong side of the stocking. Pin, then stitch the upper raw edges of the cuff and stocking together. Turn the cuff to the outside of the stocking.

## Stamping the bag

1 Make a paper template from the bag on page 33, then cut two bag pieces from the purple dupion. Stamp the small crown using gold paint on to one bag piece, see page 33 for position. Leave to dry, then fix as before.

2 To make the ribbon hanger: sew a folded length of thin blue ribbon to the top of the bag. With right sides facing and taking 1cm (³⁄₈in) seam allowance, stitch the bag pieces together. Snip the curves and turn right side out. Press under 6mm (¹⁄₄in) on the upper edges then a further 6mm (¹⁄₄in) and stitch in place. Tie a bow of red ribbon around the bag.

## Stamping the heart pouch

1 Make a paper template of the heart on page 34, then cut two hearts from the red card. Paint the small holly leaf stamp with embossing paint and press firmly on one paper heart. Stamp a second heart, then before the paint dries, sprinkle gold embossing powder on the ink. Shake off the excess.

2 Hold the paper heart over a heated toaster for a few seconds to melt the embossing powder (see Stamping Techniques, page 11).

3 Glue the two paper hearts together at the edges, leaving the top open. Glue a tassel from the centre bottom, a jewellery stone between the embossed leaves and thin red ribbon to the top for hanging the heart. Wrap a gift in tissue paper and slip inside the heart.

## Stamping the crown pouch

1 Make the crown pouch from gold card, in the same way as the red heart. Use embossing ink to stamp curls, which are then embossed with blue powder. Glue a jewellery stone at the bottom of the curls, then finish with red ribbon and blue tissue paper.

## Stamping the seat cover

1 Make a plan of your chair seat like the one on page 32, adding 1cm (³⁄₈in) to all sides for turnings. You will need to cut two seat covers from the blue dupion and one from felt.

2 Lay one seat cover flat on your work table. Stamp with the four parts of the large dove, centrally on to one of the seat covers. Leave to dry, then fix with an iron. Tack the felt to the reverse side of the stamped cover.

3 Cut four strips of purple dupion for ties, each approximately 60x15cm (24x6in) in length. Fold each tie in half lengthways and stitch along the long and one short edge. Snip the corners and turn right side out. Press the ties, tack across the raw ends.

4 Tack the ties to the back corners of the stamped cover, following diagram 1 on page 32, so that when tied they will hold the cover on to the seat.

5 Make a paper pattern of the chair skirt design on page 35, adding enough sections to fit around the sides and front of the seat cover. On the outer edges, add the extra fabric

shown as shaded areas on the diagram. From the red dupion cut two chair skirts. Make another skirt for the back edge of the chair. If the skirts are not exactly the same size as the chair seat, leave gaps at the sides of the legs.

6 Lay one of the skirts on to your work table and stamp with the large holly leaf, using gold paint on to each point of the skirt. Leave to dry then fix with the iron.

7 Pin the two chair skirts together right sides facing, then stitch together, taking a 1cm (³/₈in) seam allowance leaving a gap at the top edge for turning. Trim the seam allowance at the points and snip to the inner corners. Turn right side out through the gap. Press then sew up the gap. Repeat for the back chair skirt.

9 With right sides facing, tack one skirt to the side and front edges of the stamped cover and one to the back, see diagram 2 below. Fold in the ties and skirts and with right sides facing, place the un-stamped seat cover over the stamped seat, enclosing the skirts and the leg ties. Taking a 1cm (³/₈in) seam allowance, stitch around the seat cover, leaving a 25cm (10in) gap on the back edge for turning see diagram 3 below. Turn right side out, then slipstitch the gap.

10 Sew a bead to each point on the two skirts, then slip stitch a thick gold cord along the seam between the skirt and the seat cover. Place the cover over the chair, loop the ties a couple of times around the chair legs and tie in bows.

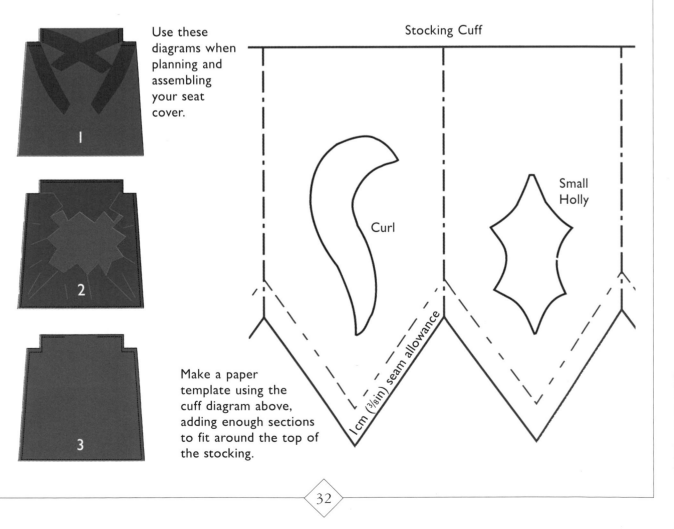

Use these diagrams when planning and assembling your seat cover.

1

2

3

Make a paper template using the cuff diagram above, adding enough sections to fit around the top of the stocking.

Stocking Cuff

Curl

1cm (³/₈in) seam allowance

Small Holly

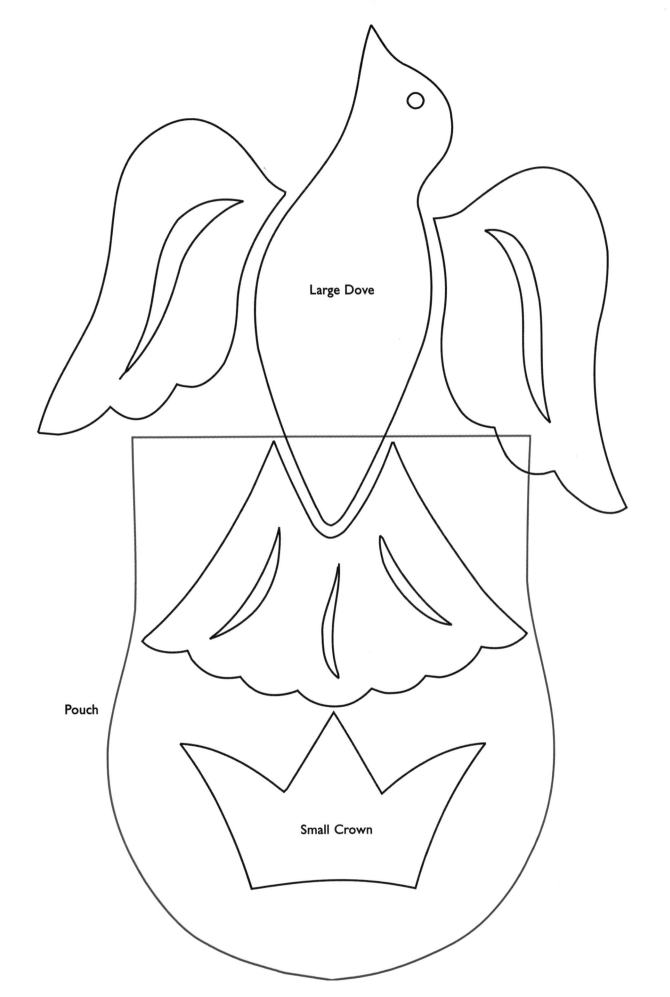

Large Dove

Pouch

Small Crown

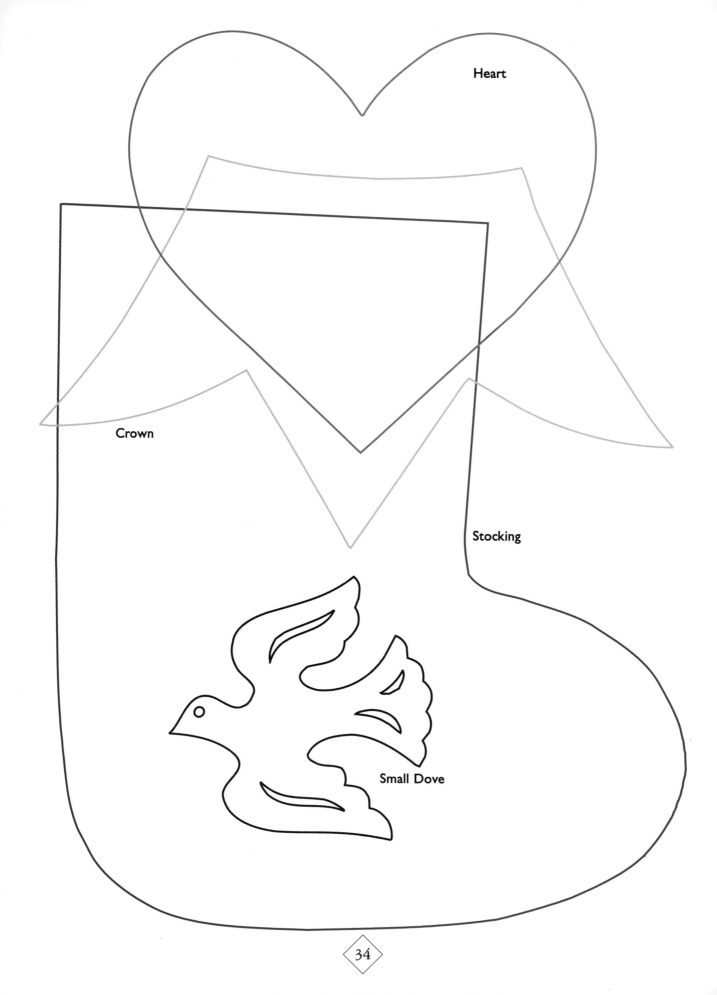

Heart

Crown

Stocking

Small Dove

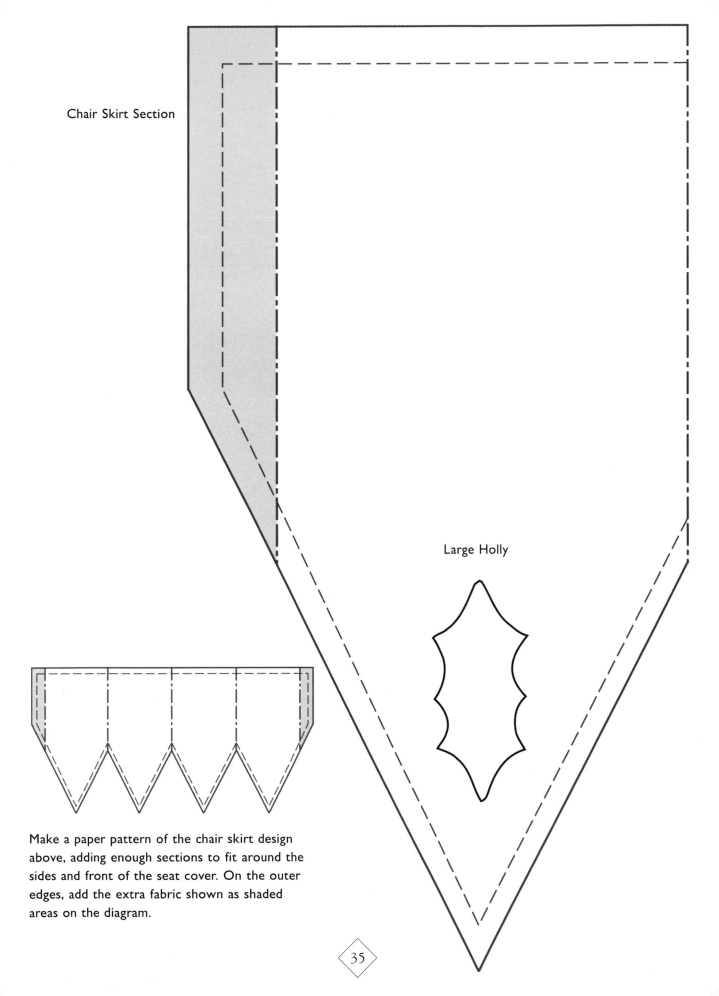

Chair Skirt Section

Large Holly

Make a paper pattern of the chair skirt design above, adding enough sections to fit around the sides and front of the seat cover. On the outer edges, add the extra fabric shown as shaded areas on the diagram.

# Fleur-de-Lys

Fleur-de-lys (or iris flower) is an image often associated with heraldry; used on many coat-of-arms, it will bring a regal feel to even the plainest cotton fabric. Printed in lime green, with a silver dotted background pattern the fleur-de-lys has been brought right up to date in this stylish project

## You will need

- Cotton fabric medium weight (not chintz or satin) 1.3mx90cm(1³⁄₈ydx45in) – white
- Coolie lampshade frame 25cm (10in) diameter
- Cushion pad 38cm (15in) square
- Three skeins of pearl cotton No 5 – lime green
- Fabric paint – yellow, green, dark brown, silver
- Sewing thread – white
- Tape or bias binding 12mm (¹⁄₂in) – white
- Polystyrene tile 5mm (¹⁄₄in) thick
- Mounting card 10cm (4in) square
- Masking tape 2.5cm (1in), double-sided tape
- Medium stencil brush, all-purpose glue
- Craft knife, cutting board, scissors
- Soft pencil, felt-tipped pen, ball-point pen
- White paper, brown paper, kitchen paper
- Pins, wooden clothes peg, teaspoon, small jar
- Cocktail sticks, flat dish for mixing paint
- Iron, fluffy towel

## Making the stamp

1 Trace off the shapes 1 to 4 of the fleur-de-lys motif on page 41 on to white paper with a soft pencil. Secure the tracing to mounting card and using a ball-point pen, draw over the outlines, pressing hard enough to mark the mounting card. Remove the tracing and draw over the lines on the mounting card. Cut out the card shapes then stick to the polystyrene tile with double-sided tape. Cut out the tile shapes.

2 Using the same method as before, trace the exact layout of the stamp, including the dotted positioning lines on to another piece of polystyrene tile.

3 Stick the cut-out shapes, card side up, directly on top of the outlines on the polystyrene tile, using double-sided tape.

4 Trim the polystyrene so it is about 1cm (³⁄₈in) away from the shapes.

5 Using a ball-point pen, extend the positioning lines around the edges of the polystyrene to the flat side.

## Preparing the fabric

1 Wrap a sheet of brown paper around the lampshade frame, overlap the edges and hold them together with small pieces of

masking tape. Mark the outer edges of the top and bottom rings and one of the struts on to the paper; for the lining, repeat this process inside the lampshade. Add approximately 2.5cm (1in) to all edges for seams.

2 Wash and partially dry the fabric, then press whilst still damp. On the fabric, mark out the following shapes using a soft pencil; two 50cm (20in) squares, for the cushion; one piece 18x56cm (7x22in), for the bag; and two pieces, using the paper patterns as guides, for the lampshade.

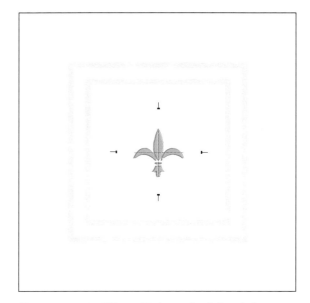

Position a pin 7.5cm (3in) to the left of the centre point of the cushion front; repeat to the right, above and below. Place masking tape 7.5cm (3in) from the outermost points of the motif to form a square. Make another square 1.5cm (1/2in) outside the first.

3 Find the centre of one of the cushion pieces, then position a pin 7.5cm (3in) to the left of the centre point; repeat to the right, above and below. When stamping these four pins will line-up with the positioning lines marked on the back of the stamp.

4 For the bag: fold the rectangle in half widthways. On one half of the fabric, using a pin, mark a point 4cm (1½in) above the folded edge; 15cm (6in) above this place another pin, then midway between the pins, mark the centre point. Place pins to the left and right, each 7.5cm (3in) from the centre point.

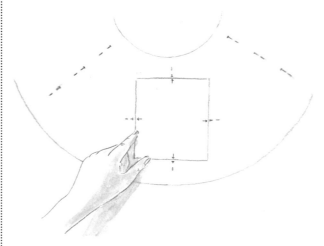

5 Fold the lampshade outer paper pattern into thirds and transfer these folded lines to the fabric using pins. Across the top of the fabric mark the central position of each section. On the bottom mark a position 2.5cm (1in) up from the bottom edge, excluding the seam allowance. Place the dry stamp on the fabric, lining the pins up with the positioning lines on the stamp.

## Applying the stamp

1 Pour about three quarters of the yellow fabric paint into a jar and add a drop of green. Dip a cocktail stick into the dark brown then mix with the green mix; repeat for the yellow then mix thoroughly. Adjust the colour by adding more green, brown or yellow paint.

2 Apply the lime green paint to the stamp using a brush and covering the card evenly. Stamp the motif in the middle of the cushion

front, on the bag and three times on the lampshade fabric, aligning the positioning lines on the stamp with the pin marks on the fabric. Add more paint to the stamp between each application. If the stamp begins to get clogged with paint, clean the surface with cotton wool dipped in water. Dry thoroughly before re-applying the paint, and continuing with the stamping. Leave to dry.

## Adding the decoration

1 On the cushion front place a strip of masking tape about 7.5cm (3in) from the outermost points of the fleur-de-lys motif on each side to form a square. Take care to make neat corner points. Repeat, making another square 1.5cm (½in) outside the first, see the diagram on page 38.

2 Using a stencil brush, or a paintbrush: paint with a dabbing motion between the strips of masking tape using lime green paint. Leave to dry. Remove the masking tape strips.

3 Shake the silver paint well, then pour into a dish. Cut one of the pointed ends off a cocktail stick. Dip the blunt end of the stick into the silver paint at the edge, where the paint has slightly dried. Using the diagram on page 41 as a guide, dot the silver paint on to the fabric in groups of three, filling the background on the cushion front between the fleur-de-lys motif and the border. Use the same guide to fill the background bag fabric.

4 On the lampshade fabric the rows of dots have to be graduated: start with the bottom

row of dots, these should be positioned approximately 2.5cm (1in) up from the bottom edge of the fabric, excluding the seam allowance. Each group of dots should be positioned 3.8cm (1½in) apart and following the curve of the fabric. Place the next row approximately 2.5cm (1in) up from the first but with smaller gaps between each group of dots. On the third row remove every third or fourth group of dots so that the gaps are not less than 2cm (¾in). Continue reducing the space between the groups of dots, until all the background fabric has been covered.

5 Take the spring out of a wooden clothes peg, then dip the blunt wooden end into the silver paint. Stamp the collar (shape 5 of the diagram on page 41), on each fleur-de-lys.

6 Leave to dry flat, then place the fabric face down on a fluffy towel and iron to fix the paint (see Fixing Fabric Paint, page 13).

## Finishing the cushion

1 Trim the cushion front and back to size, adding a 1.5cm (½in) seam allowance to all edges. With right sides together pin, tack, then stitch the two pieces around three sides of the cushion, and just in from the corners on the fourth side. Neaten the seams, clip the seam allowance around the corners, then remove tacking. Press, then turn the cover right side out.

2 For a 38cm (15in) cushion pad, make a cord using ten 4.3m (4¾yd) lengths of pearl cotton. To estimate the length required: measure around the four sides of the finished cushion, add 5cm (2in) for each corner loop, plus 7.5cm (3in), then multiply by 2.5.

3 Place all the lengths of cotton thread together and knot both ends. Secure one

end to a hook or door knob. Place a pencil between the strands at the other end, then twist the pencil round and round keeping the strands taught, until they are very tightly twisted together. Still keeping the strands taught bring the two knotted ends together and tie: the cord will now twist-up further, even out the twists removing any kinks.

4 Pin the cord evenly around the sides of the cushion. Follow the seam line, making a loop at each corner and placing the ends of the cord in the centre of the open side. Stitch the cord to the edge of the cushion, using small neat slip stitches.

5 Insert the cushion pad. Pin then stitch up the opening, using small neat slip stitches, enclosing the ends of the cord within the cushion.

## Finishing the herb bag

1 With right sides together, fold the printed rectangle of fabric in half lengthways. Pin, tack, then stitch the side seams together, taking a 1.5cm (½in) seam allowance. Neaten the seams, then remove the tacking and press. Turn right side out, then press. Turn over the top raw edge of the bag twice and stitch in place.

2 Make a cord in the same way as for the cushion, but with four lengths of pearl cotton 1m (1⅛yd) long. When finished, tie a neat knot at each end and trim off any surplus cord. Tie the cord around the top of the bag, finishing with a bow.

## Finishing the lampshade

1 Bind the top and bottom rings of the lampshade with tape or bias binding. Sew over the ends to secure the tape. With right sides together pin, tack, then stitch the two

short straight sides on the printed lampshade fabric together. Neaten the seam, then remove tacking. Turn right side out and press the seam. Repeat with the lining fabric but do not turn fabric.

2 Place the printed cover over the frame and pin to the tape on the bottom and top rings: pull the fabric slightly taught to remove wrinkles. Sew the fabric to the tape using small slanting stitches as near to the outside edges of the rings as possible. Trim the surplus fabric close to the stitches.

3 Insert the lining cover inside the frame and pin the fabric in the same way as the outer cover. Make two small cuts in the lining where the struts are connected to the top ring. Turn under the cut edges, then attach the lining at the top and bottom edges. Trim away any surplus fabric.

4 Cut a strip of fabric approximately 2x15cm (³/₄x6in) long. Turn over the long edges, press, then cut the strip in two. Working inside the lampshade, place the middle of one strip under a strut. Fold the ends over the top ring; pin, then stitch to cover the cut made for the strut. Trim away any surplus fabric at the top edge. Repeat with the other strut.

5 Make four twisted cords, each from four lengths of pearl cotton: two for the top of the shade and two for the bottom. Cut eight lengths 1.1m (1¹/₄yd) and eight 2.3m (2.5yd).

6 Pin one of the shorter cords around the top of the lampshade and glue in place. To neaten the cord ends: place glue on the cord where you want to cut. Allow to dry, then cut. Glue the cord ends in position. Repeat with the other short cord placing it below the first. Repeat with the bottom edge.

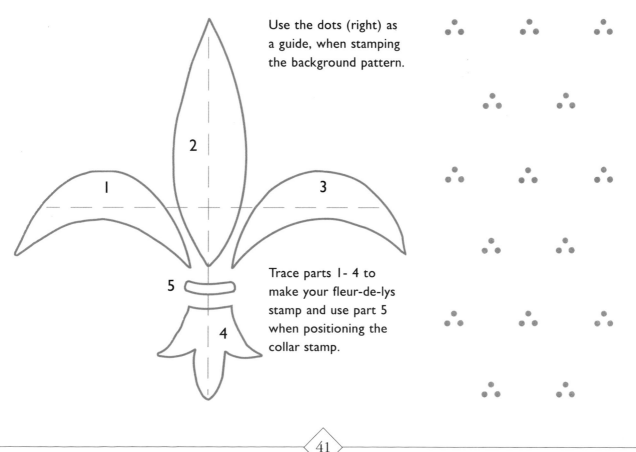

Use the dots (right) as a guide, when stamping the background pattern.

Trace parts 1- 4 to make your fleur-de-lys stamp and use part 5 when positioning the collar stamp.

# Lazy Daisy

Have fun brightening up your home without spending a fortune, with these charming blue daisies. The stamps, made from recycled materials like packing foam and corks, will cost you next to nothing to make, and can be used to brighten up paper, fabric, wood or even a terracotta plant pot

## You will need

- Lampshade – cream
- Lining paper
- Terracotta plant pot
- Writing paper and envelopes – cream
- Wooden coat hook
- Sheet packing foam 2mm (1/16in) – white
- Small blocks of wood
- Bottle corks
- Acrylic paint – blue, yellow
- Felt-tipped pen, thick nib – navy blue
- Matt emulsion paint – cream
- Matt acrylic varnish
- Masking tape 2.5cm (1in), double-sided tape
- Cutting mat, cutting board, sharp craft scissors, felt-tipped pen
- White paper, ball-point pen, metal ruler, pencil, rubber eraser
- Flat dish for mixing paint, kitchen paper, fine sandpaper
- Decorator's brush, paintbrush
- PVA glue, damp cloth

## Making the stamp

1 If you are thinking of embarking on a large amount of stamping, such as a complete room frieze, it will save time at the stamping stage if you prepare several stamps before you begin. Although the packing foam is strong, the glue holding the petals on to the wood will begin to breakdown after prolonged stamping.

2 Select a block of wood to make the small and large daisy stamp: it should be large enough for the petals to be arranged in a circle on one side of the wood. Using fine sandpaper, rub down the top surface of the block. Wipe away the dust with a damp cloth, then leave to dry.

3 Trace off the two petal shapes on page 45 on to white paper with a ball-point pen; make several spare templates to give you replacements if the originals get worn or damaged. Cut out the paper shapes accurately using small craft scissors.

4 Lay a sheet of packing foam on the cutting mat; on top place the small paper template. Hold the template on to the foam with one finger, and using a thin black felt-tipped pen, draw around the petal shape. Repeat across the sheet, replacing the paper template if it gets worn. Repeat for the large template. Using sharp craft scissors, cut out the foam petals.

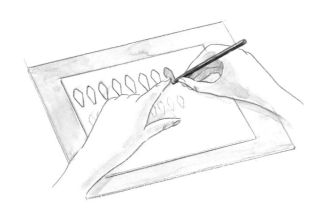

5 Following the diagram on page 45, stick eight petals firmly on to the top surface of the wooden block, forming a circle: leave enough space in the centre for a cork to be stamped. Repeat for the other stamp.

## Preparing the frieze

1 Measure the wall to find the length of frieze needed. Measure, then cut the lining paper to the same length. Lay the lining paper on a flat, surface. Unroll about 1m (39in) of paper.

2 Using a metal ruler, measure up 1cm (³/₈in) from the bottom of the paper and draw a faint pencil line along the length of the paper; measure up from this line 3cm (1¹/₄in) and mark another faint line, and again 3cm (1¹/₄in) above the last; finally mark the top cutting line 1cm (³/₈in) above this, see the diagram on the opposite page.

3 To cut the frieze: re-roll the paper and then lay the beginning of the roll on to a cutting mat. Using a sharp knife and metal ruler, cut along the length of the paper on the furthest pencil line from the bottom paper edge.

4 Starting at the beginning of the frieze, make a pencil mark every 5cm (2in) along the central pencil line. These marks will be the centre points of the stamped flowers.

5 To draw the decorative lines: re-roll the frieze and using a thick, blue felt-tipped pen and a metal ruler, draw along the two outer pencil lines: use the longest ruler you can find, lifting the felt-tipped pen from the paper as infrequently as possible.

## Stamping the frieze

1 Unroll the frieze, to give the longest working length that space will allow.

2 Put a small quantity of blue acrylic paint in a dish, and using a paintbrush apply the paint to the foam area of the larger stamp.

3 Press the stamp on to the paper, on the first marked position on the central pencil line.

4 Load the small stamp with paint and apply the stamp to the next marked position. Continue with alternate sizes along the length of the paper. Leave the paint to dry before moving on to complete the next section.

5 Using the thick blue felt-tipped pen, make a mark at the centre point of each flower.

## Stamping the lampshade

1 Turn the lampshade upside down, then position the dry stamp on to the lampshade. Using a pencil, mark the bottom corners of the wooden block on to the edge of the shade, with a small faint pencil mark.

2 Continue marking around the shade until you get to the last position, you will find that it is smaller or larger than needed for the stamp. Use the rubber eraser to remove the pencil marks, then re-mark the positions, making the spaces of an equal size.

3 Using a paintbrush, load the stamp with blue paint; then press the stamp on to the

shade between the first two pencil marks, lining the bottom of the stamp up with the bottom of the shade. Continue stamping around the bottom of the lampshade in this way.

4 Using a paintbrush, load the end of a small cork with yellow paint. Press the cork on to the lampshade in the middle of each flower.

## Stamping the terracotta pot

1 Scrub the terracotta pot in warm soapy water to remove any dust or marks. Leave to dry overnight.

2 Use the large and small stamps to make patterns on the surface of the pot; finish with cork stamped yellow centres and use the paint brush to paint a line around the top.

## Stamping the coat hook

1 Using fine sandpaper, rub down the surface of the wooden coat hook. Wipe with a damp cloth, then leave to dry. Apply two or three coats of matt emulsion paint, leaving to dry for several hours between coats.

2 Stamp daisies on the surface of the wood in blue, using the cork to add yellow centres. Stamp on to the flat end of the hangers with a cork, loaded with blue paint. Leave to dry, then paint with two coats of matt acrylic varnish.

## Stamping the paper

1 For the wrapping paper: stamp large blue daisies with yellow centres randomly over a sheet of lining paper. Position them very close together, overlapping some of the petals.

2 For the writing paper: using the small daisy, stamp a single flower with a blue centre on each sheet of paper.

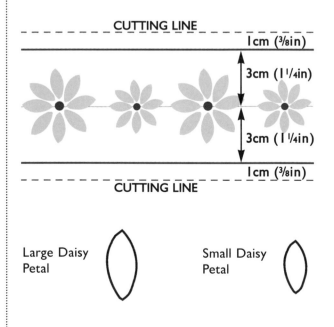

**CUTTING LINE**

1cm (³⁄₈in)

3cm (1¹⁄₄in)

3cm (1¹⁄₄in)

1cm (³⁄₈in)

**CUTTING LINE**

Large Daisy Petal

Small Daisy Petal

Trace off the petal outlines above to make your daisy stamp, then use the diagram to position the petals on the stamp and create your wall frieze.

# Hand Printing

If you like getting your hands dirty and getting stuck into a craft project, then this is the technique for you. Use your own hands as stamps; or if you prefer make hand stamped shapes from potatoes. Whatever method you choose you are sure to have great fun making these creative winter accessories

## You will need

- White gloves, scarf, hat and socks
- Black velvet hat and gloves
- Ivory polyester fabric – 50x112cm (20x45in)
- Coloured felt – two pieces 28x28cm (11x11in) bag back and front, three pieces 28x7.5cm (11x3in) bag gussets, two pieces 56x7.5cm (22x3in) bag handles, one piece 20x28cm (8x11in) bag flap
- Fabric paint – white, black, yellow, pink, light blue, red
- Iron-on fabric stiffener
- Stranded cotton – blue, large eyed needle
- Two large baking potatoes, kitchen paper, pins
- Cutting board, kitchen knife, scissors, masking tape
- Paintbrush, dish for mixing paint
- Felt-tipped pen, pencil, white paper
- Iron, fluffy towel

## Making the scarf

1 To make the scarf: cut the polyester fabric in half widthways. Turn the edges of the fabric over, twice. Tack, then with large blanket stitch; or you may prefer to zig-zag the edges using a sewing machine.

## Hand stamping the scarf

1 Lay the scarf on a paper covered flat surface, and secure with pieces of masking tape.

2 You will need to find dishes that are large enough to get the flat area of your hand on to. Polystyrene trays that hold fresh produce are ideal and can be thrown away when they get dirty. Mix together the black and white fabric paint in varying proportions on the mixing dish, creating light grey and dark grey colours – these should be mixed in separate dishes. Place the dishes in a convenient position next to the material, then roll up your sleeves. Have kitchen paper handy, so that you can wipe your hands easily (see Using Your Hands, page 9).

3 Place your left hand in one dish of paint and your right hand in the other, making sure every part of your hand is well covered. Press one hand firmly on the fabric, then carefully remove. Press the other hand firmly on the fabric, then remove. Practice to get accustomed to the process.

4 Now start printing on the material working from the top downwards, re-applying the paint to your hands between each application. If you place your hand-prints close enough together, you should manage to produce seven pairs of hands down the length of each scarf.

5 Stamp the multi-coloured scarf using the same method. Place your hands in the first two colours then stamp the design on the scarf, washing and drying your hands to add the third colour. Let your hands touch, overlap and even run off the edge of the scarf for effect.

6 Leave to dry then fix by placing the fabric face down on a fluffy towel and ironing for 1-2 minutes on the hottest setting suitable for the fabric. Iron the polyester scarf on a silk setting.

## Making the potato stamp

1 On white paper using a pencil, make tracings of the hand and foot shape of your choice, from the diagrams on pages 50 and 51. Cut out the six pieces for each hand or foot separately, using scissors.

2 On a cutting board and using a sharp vegetable knife, cut a large firm baking potato in half lengthways. Dry the cut surface

of the potato, then place it cut side down on kitchen paper to soak up any excess fluid. Pin the paper tracings for either the hand or the foot shape on to the surface of the potato: use a dressmaker's pin to hold it firmly to the surface by pushing the pin straight down in to the potato. Draw around the outer edge of the shape with felt-tipped pen.

3 With a small kitchen knife cut away the potato outside of the design lines, to a depth of approximately 1cm (³/₈in). Cut the potato in small sections, gently sculpting around the finger and toe shapes. The potatoes will ooze liquid while you cut, this should be mopped up with kitchen paper. When you have finished cutting lay the potato cut side down on kitchen paper, to soak up any excess fluid.

## Stamping with a potato

1 Pour paint on to your mixing dish, then with a paintbrush spread paint over the surface of the dish. For each application, dip the cut side of the potato into the paint; or apply the paint using the brush. If you are working on a large area of fabric, it will be quicker and easier to dip the potato in the paint; but if you want greater control over the

thickness of the paint, apply it with a paint-brush. Test the first few applications on paper, to ensure all the liquid has soaked out of the potato.

2 Lay the black velvet hat on a clean work surface. Cut rough paper masks to cover the areas of the hat not being stamped: this will protect them from paint splashes. Load the potato hand stamp with silver metallic paint and press on to fabric, around the rim of the hat.

3 Lay the black gloves on the work surface, stretch out the fabric, then stick the gloves to the work surface with masking tape. Using

the same potato stamp as for the hat, stamp hands on to the back on the gloves.

4 Attach the white gloves and socks to your work surface with masking tape, then decorate with the potato stamped hand shapes using pink, light blue and yellow fabric paint. If you have trouble cleaning the paint from the surface of the potato between colours, it may be easier to cut a new stamp for each colour.

5 Attach the felt fabric pieces cut for the bag to your work surface with masking tape. Using a brush, paint pink fabric paint on the palm and fingers of the potato hand stamp, and red for the finger nails.

6 Leave the stamped fabric, gloves, socks and hat to dry, then fix by placing face down on a fluffy towel and ironing for 1-2 minutes on the hottest setting suitable for the fabric. Take great care when ironing the velvet: if the iron is too hot it will flatten the pile.

## Finishing the hat

1 To finish the black velvet hat: wrap a stamped scarf loosely around the crown, tying the ends in a bow.

## Making the felt bag

1 Lay the stamped and fixed felt, design side down on a flat surface. Iron the stiffener on to the felt, then cut away any excess stiffener.

2 Pin the gusset strips to the three sides of the large felt squares. Using a large-eyed needle threaded with all six strands of stranded cotton, and starting at the top, stitch around all seams in a large blanket stitch. Cut a flap the same size as the width of the bag, cutting away the bottom edge to form a point. Tack the flap to the top of the bag, finishing with large blanket stitches. To make a handle: blanket stitch the two lengths of felt together along the long sides, then blanket stitch the handles to the top edge of gusset.

In addition to using your own hands to stamp, make potato stamps by tracing off the hand or foot shapes of your choice from the diagrams opposite.

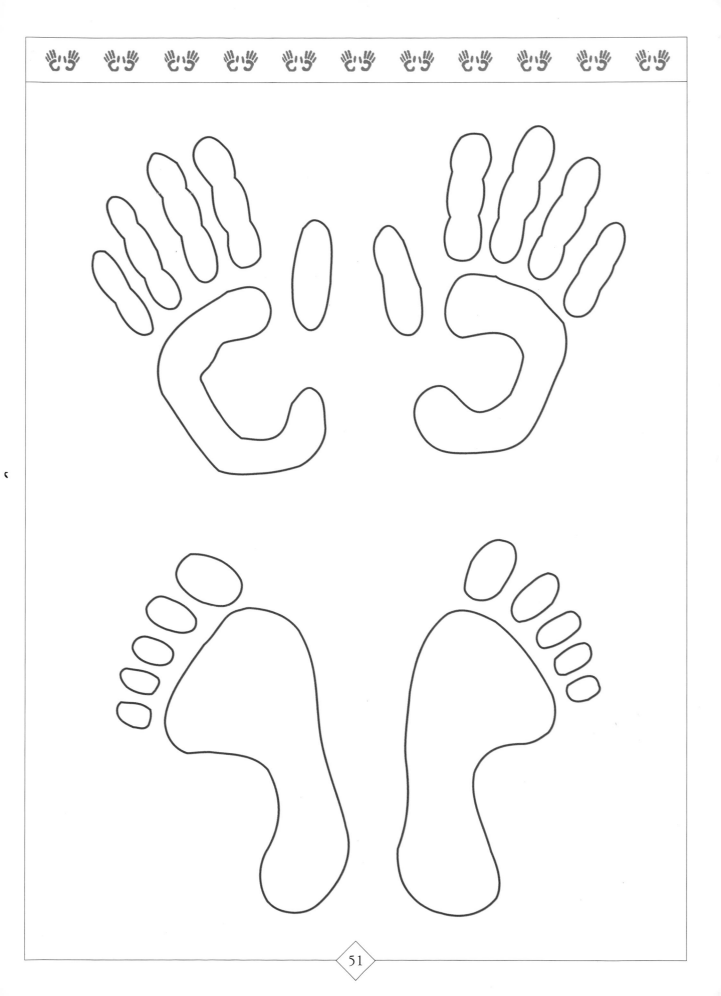

# Checkerboard Chest and Box

Rather than packing your Christmas decorations away, store them in this useful drawer stack or box stamped with simple shapes made from a washing-up sponge. Raid the cupboard under the sink for that pack of sponges and get snipping – a great excuse not to do the dishes!

The tree decorations are inexpensive to make from off-cuts of wood; or you could use children's building blocks, which are ready sanded and pre-painted needing fewer coats of paint to get a good stamping surface.

## You will need
- Small wooden chest of drawers
- Wooden box
- Wooden off-cuts or children's building blocks – cube shaped
- Acrylic paint – cream, bright green, turquoise, blue, silver, red, green
- Washing-up sponge – synthetic
- Flat dish for paint, decorator's paintbrush, container of clean water, fine sandpaper
- Scrap paper, pencil, sharp scissors, chalk, pins, ruler
- Water-based brush-on satin varnish

## Preparing the chest and box

1 Remove the knobs or handles from the chest and the box. Sand the surfaces lightly to remove any rough patches of wood. Wipe the surfaces using a damp clean cloth. When dry, paint the chest of drawers with cream acrylic paint and the box with blue. You may need to thin the paint with water and apply several coats to give a good finish. Leave to dry.

## Making the stamps

1 For the checkerboard chest: measure a drawer front and draw the shape on to paper. Divide the area into squares or rectangles of an equal size, and cut out to create your stamp templates.

2 Pin one of the squares or rectangles on to the washing-up sponge. Using sharp scissors, carefully cut the sponge to the same size as the template to create a stamp (see Making Stamps, page 8). You will need to make a sponge stamp for each of the colours used. Two stamps are required for the drawer fronts: one for the turquoise and one for the green. (Note: The cream squares are the original base colour of the chest of drawers.)

3 A slightly larger sponge stamp was used to decorate the chest top and sides. Measure the area, divide up the paper shape, then make sponge shapes for each of the paint colours.

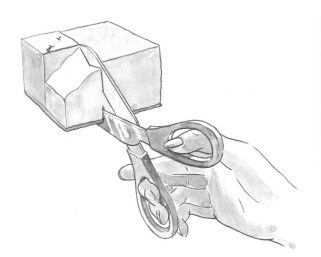

4 For the box: you will need two square sponge stamps. To make these, draw two 3cm (1¼in) squares on paper and cut out. Pin the paper squares to the washing-up sponge and cut out.

5 Trace the larger Christmas tree template on page 55, cut out and pin to the washing-up sponge. Cut out the tree shape.

## Stamping the drawers

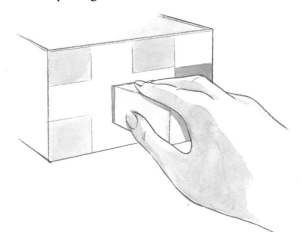

1 Use two stamps (one for each colour) to create a checkerboard effect on the drawer fronts. Paint the colour on to the sponge stamp and press it firmly on to the surface of the drawer. Lift off the stamp, taking care not to smudge the paint. As you will be working

with a large area of wet paint, great care should be taken when positioning and removing the stamps from the surface of the wood.

2 For the sides and top of the chest, stamp with the larger sponge rectangles or squares using the same green and turquoise paint colours as on the drawer fronts.

3 Leave to dry, then apply two coats of satin varnish. Replace the knobs or handles on the drawer fronts (see Applying Varnish to Wood, page 12).

## Stamping the box

1 Load one of the square stamps cut for the box with silver paint. Stamp around the top edge of the box. You will need to apply paint to the sponge between each application. Load the second square with red paint and stamp around the bottom edge. You can either position the stamps by eye; or you may prefer to draw chalk lines around the box to line up with the top or bottom edge of the stamp.

2 Load the tree stamp with green paint and stamp in a row between the silver and red squares.

3 Leave to dry, then apply two coats of satin varnish.

## Stamping the decorations

1 Use wood off-cuts or children's building blocks to make the decorations: paint with two coats of cream, blue or red paint, then leave to dry. Cut stamps from the foam in the same way as for the chest or box, using the smaller Christmas tree shape for the decorations. Stamp the blocks; leave to dry, then paint with two coats of satin varnish. Tie-up like a parcel with silver elastic ribbon, leaving a loop at the top for hanging.

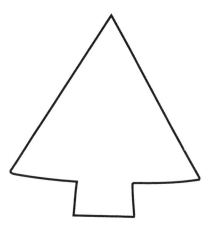

Use these shapes to make stamps for decorating your own Christmas box and tree ornaments.

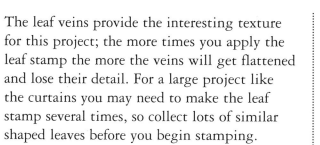

# Leaf Cushion and Curtains

Why not let nature provide the equipment for your project? This pretty fabric was stamped using real leaves, then made into curtains and a cushion. You could use almost any leaf for this project, collected in the garden or on a country walk. So start now, before your stamps get blown away on the wind

The leaf veins provide the interesting texture for this project; the more times you apply the leaf stamp the more the veins will get flattened and lose their detail. For a large project like the curtains you may need to make the leaf stamp several times, so collect lots of similar shaped leaves before you begin stamping.

## You will need

- Cotton sheeting – white
- Cushion pad 28x28cm (11x11in)
- Curtain heading tape
- White cotton sewing thread
- Fabric paint – pink, bright green
- Fresh leaves
- Lining paper, masking tape
- Mount board or card, ball-point pen
- PVA glue
- Foam roller, flat dish for paint
- Iron, clean cloth

## Preparing the fabric

1 Wash, dry and press the cotton sheeting fabric, this will remove any 'finishing' from the surface of the fabric.

2 For the cushion cover: cut two 48cm (19in) squares of fabric. For the curtains: measure the window and cut the fabric allowing extra for turnings at the top and bottom. Depending on the size of your window, you may need to join several widths of fabric together. Allow at least twice the width of your window in fabric fullness.

3 For the curtains: cut lining paper strips 18cm (7in) wide and the length of the fabric – these will act as guides when placed on the fabric. The distance left between the strips should be the width of your leaf plus a small amount. Hold the paper in place with small pieces of masking tape. This will give you a straight edge to follow when stamping and protect the fabric not being painted.

4 Always test the paint on the fabric before you begin stamping: some fabrics soak-up the paint more rapidly than others, so your test will help you load the stamp with the correct quantity of paint. Some paints will 'bleed' into the fabric: if this happens thicken the fabric paint with a little stencil paint of a similar colour. Through trial and error you will

discover how much paint to apply in order to give the effect you desire.

## Making the leaf stamp

1 Place the leaf top side down on to mount board or card. Using a ball-point pen, trace around the outside of the leaf. Remove the leaf and cut out the leaf shape inside the drawn lines, so that the card is very slightly smaller than the leaf. Glue the top side of the leaf to the card shape (see Making Stamps, page 8). You will be using the underside of the leaf as a stamp, as the veins on the leaf are more pronounced on the back. Glue a small piece of mount board to the card leaf shape to act as a handle.

## Applying the leaf stamp

1 Cover your work table with lining paper then lay your prepared fabric (see Preparing the Fabric, on the previous page), out flat on the surface.

2 You will be working on one strip at a time – leave the paint to dry before moving on to the next strip. Pour the green fabric paint into the paint tray, load the roller with paint and roll over the surface of the leaf stamp covering it evenly with paint. Press the stamp down on to the fabric in the correct position,

lift off the fabric taking care not to spread the paint. You may find that you need to load the stamp with paint between each application. The markings on the leaf will lessen each time you use the stamp: make a new stamp when you feel the detail on the leaf is becoming faint.

3 For the cushion cover: stamp around the outside edges of both squares of fabric, leaving at least 2.5cm (1in) around the edge for turnings.

4 When the paint is dry fix the colour by covering the fabric with a clean cotton cloth. Iron for 1-2 minutes on the hottest setting suitable for the fabric.

## Making-up the cushion

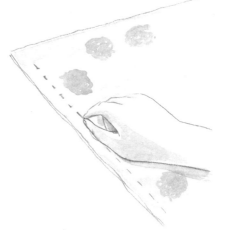

1 To make the cushion cover: place the two squares of material right sides together, pin and tack 1.5cm (⅝in) from the edge. Machine stitch following the tacking line around three sides, leaving a 25cm (10in) opening on one side. Trim the seams and turn the cover through to the right side.

2 Measure 10cm (4in) in from the outside edges and draw a line lightly with a dressmaker's pencil around the four sides of the

cover. Pin, tack and machine stitch on this line on three sides, this will make a pocket inside the cover. Insert the pad in the pocket then pin, tack and machine stitch along the fourth side to hold the pad in place. Close the opening on the edge of the cover with small neat stitches. Add a line of machine stitching diagonally in each corner of the cover, from the corner of the pad to the outside corner of the cover.

**3** To assemble the curtains: turn under the side edges of each curtain and machine stitch in place. Attach curtain tape to the top of the curtains, then turn-up the bottom and hem in place.

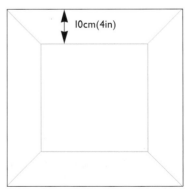

10cm(4in)

To stitch the detail markings on the cushion cover: measure 10cm (4in) in from the outer edge of the fabric, mark a square on the fabric. Stitch around the square and diagonally from each corner of the square to the corners of the cushion cover.

# Spiral Pots and Cards

If you have ever wondered what to do with the paint left over from a decorating spree, then this is the project for you. Alternatively you can buy tester pots of paint, which will give you enough paint to finish a few terracotta pots and stamp a selection of greetings cards

## You will need

- For the pots: terracotta plant pots
- For the cards: coloured card – green, blue, yellow; textured paper – green, yellow, pink
- Emulsion paint – green, blue, yellow, pink
- Thick string, corrugated card
- Craft knife, cutting board, scissors, ruler
- All-purpose glue
- Paintbrush

### Preparing the pots

1 Wash the pots to remove any dust or marks, then allow to dry. Paint the pots with two coats of emulsion paint. Leave to dry.

### Preparing the stamps

1 Draw a freehand spiral and coil on to corrugated card; or trace the outlines opposite on to white paper with a pencil. Lay the tracing on top of corrugated card, then draw over the lines with a ball-point pen, transferring them to the card. Glue along the design lines on the card, then lay string over the glue. Cut off the excess string. Cut the card around the outer edge of the string design, leaving a 6mm (¹/₄in) margin.

### Stamping the pot and paper

1 Paint the top of the string liberally with emulsion paint, then press firmly on to the pot. Stamp the textured paper in the same way. Leave to dry.

### Assembling the greetings card

1 To achieve the torn edge effect on the textured paper: hold a ruler firmly on the paper at one side of the design and tear away the excess paper. Repeat on the other sides.

2 Fold a piece of coloured card in half to make a card. Glue the textured paper to the front of the card.

# Acknowledgements

Thanks to the designers for contributing such wonderful projects:
Fruit Printed Bags and Paper (page 14), Janet Bridge
Trains, Boats and Planes Quilt (page 18), Lynn Strange
Fishy Tiles (page 24), Marion Elliot
Harlequin Christmas (page 28), Cheryl Owen
Fleur-de-lys (page 36), Annabelle Sheldrick
Lazy Daisy (page 42), Susan and Martin Penny
Hand Printing (page 46), Amanda Davidson
Checkerboard Chest and Box (page 52), Cheryl Owen
Leaf Cushion and Curtains (page 56), Maria Saunderson
Spiral Pots and Cards (page 60), Cheryl Owen

Many thanks to Ashton James and Jon Stone for their inspirational photography and
Doreen Holland for using her considerable needlework skills to make up projects.

## Other books in the Made Easy series

Stencilling (David & Charles, 1998)

Glass Painting (David & Charles, 1998)

Silk Painting (David & Charles, 1998)

# Suppliers

Craft Creations Ltd
Ingersoll House
Delamare Road
Cheshunt EN8 9ND
Tel: 01992 781900
Mail order service
(Paper manufacturers: card blanks, mounting card)

Craft World (Head office only)
No 8 North Street, Guildford
Surrey GU1 4AF
Tel: 07000 757070
Retail shops nationwide, telephone for local store
(Craft warehouse)

D M C Creative World Ltd
Pullman Road, Wigston
Leicestershire LE8 2DY
Tel: 0116 281 1040
Telephone or write for your nearest retail stockist
(Aida fabric and napkins)

Dylon International Ltd (Head office only)
Worsley Bridge Road
London SE26 5HD
Tel: 0181 663 4295
Telephone for your local retail stockist
(Fabric paint)

Hobby Crafts (Head office only)
River Court
Southern Sector
Bournemouth International Airport
Christchurch
Dorset BH23 6SE
Tel: 0800 272387 freephone
Retail shops nationwide, telephone for local store
(Craft warehouse)

Home Crafts Direct
PO Box 38
Leicester LE1 9BU
Tel: 0116 251 3139
Mail order service
(Craft equipment)

Ikea Ltd
2 Drury Way
North Circular Road
London NW10 OTH
Tel: 0181 208 5607
(Wooden boxes and furniture)
Retail shops nationwide, telephone for local store

Offray & Son Ltd (Head office only)
Fir Tree Place, Church Road
Ashford
Middlesex
TW15 2PH
Tel: 01784 247281
Telephone for your local retail stockist
(Ribbon manufacturer)

Pebeo Paints (Distributor – office address only)
Philip and Tacey Ltd
North Way
Andover
Hampshire
SP10 5BA
Tel: 01264 332171
Telephone for your local retail stockist
(Fabric paint)

Scumble Goosie
Lewiston Mill
Toadsmoor Road
Stroud
Gloucestershire
GL5 2TB
Tel: 01453 731305
Mail order service
(Wooden blanks for stamping, paint and varnish)

Squires Model & Craft Tools
The Old Corn Store
Chessels Farm, Hoe Lane
Bognor Regis
West Sussex PO22 8NW
Tel: 01243 587009
Mail order service
(Craft tools)

# Index